YAHWEH,

MY SHEPHERD AND MY KING

REVISED VERSION

RUBEN JOSEPH

To order additional copies of this book, contact:
Xlibris
844-714-8691
www.Xlibris.com
Orders@Xlibris.com

ISBN: Softcover   978-1-6641-5480-3
        EBook   978-1-6641-5479-7

Print information available on the last page

Rev. date: 09/01/2021

CONTENTS

ACKNOWLEDGMENTS

**I will bless the Lord at all times, and His praise shall
continually be in my mouth! Ps. 34:1**

My utmost gratitude and thanks go up to YHWH for giving me life, keeping me alive, and receiving me as His own. Giving up my life a thousand times over to be sacrificed for His sake would forever be inadequate to express who He is to me or repay Him for what He has done for me. He is my Shepherd, and I am forever His sheep. Amen!!!

I dedicate this book to my wonderful wife, Dr. Kédare Joseph, and my two little princesses, my pride and joy, Belle and Ruby. Thank you for being my rock and my inspiration. I love you all with all of me.

To my Dad, Tercius Joseph, and my siblings, Myrline, Stephenson, Nelcie, Judeson, Lunide, Louisenie, and Billy; and to all my relatives, thank you for your prayers and support. I love you guys!

To all my close friends who have been in my corner through thick and thin, thank you for your invaluable contributions to my life. I am forever indebted to you.

Special Thanks to Dr. Martin Klingbeil, Dr. Clifford and Dr. Josie Laguerre, Pastor Margaret Kartwe, Elder Kerby Levasseur, Commissioner Jean Monestime,

Elder Caleb Buisson, Pastor Philips Mompremier, "My Elder" Lincoln Wray, Collin and Dawn Williams, Elder Charles Cammack, Br. Jean Germeil, and all those who have invested in me over the years. May God richly bless you all!

Special Recognition: Dr. Allan Machado, Dr. Jose Joseph, Dr. Conrad Duncan, Pastor Nicolas Louis, Dr. Gervon Marsh, Pastor Eric Ampadu, and Pastor Garry Gordon.

Special thanks to Dr. Kysler Jean-Jacques—CEO of BUTLAP Firm, Haiti, for doing such a splendid job on the French translation of this book; and Pastor Joseph Mondesir, for facilitating such endeavor. I am forever indebted to you, Men of God.

FOREWORD

Martin Luther, the German protestant reformer, once commented on the Book of Psalms: "The Psalter ought to be a precious and beloved book, if for no other reason than this: it promises Christ's death and Resurrection so clearly—and pictures His kingdom and the conditions and nature of all Christendom—that it might well be called a little Bible. In it is comprehended most beautifully and briefly everything that is in the entire Bible." (Martin Luther, "Preface to the Psalter," *LW* 35, p. 254)

If indeed the Book of Psalms summarizes all of Scripture, it is Psalm 23 within this book that, like no other of its 150 poems, captures through its beautiful imagery the quintessence of the Psalms: Yahweh, my Shepherd and my King. This Davidic psalm is by far the best-known, widely-memorized, and most-recited poem in the psalter. However, sometimes familiarity breeds contempt or, even worse, indifference and while we might know a text so well, or rather, because we know a text so well, its meaning is in danger of disappearing behind the recitations and becoming mere liturgy.

This book attempts a fresh look at the imagery of Psalm 23, identifying the two guiding metaphors (plural!) of the divine Shepherd *and* King that not only reflect David's own life story but at the same time point also forward to Jesus Christ as our Shepherd and King. Ruben Joseph draws our eyes and minds towards a new engagement with the text of the poem, which will hopefully help us to follow our Divine Shepherd along still waters and green pastures, but also through death valleys, until we enter into the palace of our Divine King, where banquet tables are set, healing takes place, and a bottomless cup of mercy awaits us forever.

Martin G. Klingbeil, D.Litt.
Professor of Old Testament and Ancient Near Eastern Studies
Southern Adventist University
School of Religion

Psalm 23 is an
ageless masterpiece
filled with splendid
bucolic picturesque
imagery.

INTRODUCTION

Critical scholars suggest that all psalms originated in a cultic context. They have the same structures as the Pentateuch: Prayers, celebrations, hymns, and laments. The Hebrew Psalter presents a timeless template of prayer for all generations. The veracity of such a notion is particularly embodied in Psalm 23:

The Lord *is* my shepherd;
I shall not want.
He makes me to lie down in green pastures;
He leads me beside the still waters.
He restores my soul;
He leads me in the paths of righteousness
For His name's sake.

Yea, though I walk through the valley of the shadow of death,
I will fear no evil;
For You *are* with me;
Your rod and Your staff, they comfort me.

You prepare a table before me in the presence of my enemies;
You anoint my head with oil;

My cup runs over.
Surely goodness and mercy shall follow me
All the days of my life;
And I will dwell in the house of the Lord
Forever.

Psalm 23, according to today's scholars, is the best-known passage in the entire Old Testament (OT), by both Christians and non-Christians, and probably the most beloved in all the Psalter.

I remember Psalm 23, growing up, as being the first psalm that my siblings and I learned and memorized. Other psalms like Psalms 1, 5, 27, 46, 91, 92, and 121 were also popular in our home, but Psalm 23 was, for sure, the most recited during family worship, especially when we were in a hurry.

Coincidently, my first sermon, prepared and taught by my late Mom, was based on Psalm 23. This beautiful poem was, and still is for me, the epicenter of the Book of Psalms.

Its appeal rests in the simplicity of its formation and its poetic beauty while exuding serene confidence.[1] Psalm 23 is an ageless masterpiece filled with splendid bucolic picturesque imagery which transports the imagination far beyond the current circumstance.

The Psalm is recited in mainstream motion pictures, and in actual moments of distress—funerals, memorials, turbulences, and of course, in churches, as a liturgical part of worship.

---

[1]   Erwin Blasa and Clarence Marquez, "Towards A 'Shepherd' Spirituality: The Application of the Image of Sheep-and-Shepherd in Psalm 23 to Seminary Formation in the Philippines." *Philippiniana Sacra 45*, no. 135 (September 2010): 610–70.

It is often used as if it were a magical prayer that would automatically fix a problem—whether it be in the realm of comfort, guidance, or deliverance.

It is worth noticing that the potency of the Psalm lies not in its author nor in the beauty of its arrangement, but rather in the One to whom the Psalm is pointing—the Shepherd.

Biblical scholars arrange the book of Psalms in different categories.

Herman Gunkel, in his book, *The Psalms: A Form-Critical Introduction,* classifies Psalm 23 in the subcategory of the "Psalms of Trust." "These psalms," he notes, "reformulate the lament psalms and shift their focus to an expression of trust and confidence. . . . They often speak of Yahweh in the third person."[2] It has been my observation, however, that the Poem comprises intentional metaphors from which royal imagery may be inferred. Furthermore, Gottfried Voigt notes that the title shepherd points to the kingship of Jesus as it is a widespread notion in the Near East that the office of the shepherd is considered as a figure for royal dominion.[3]

It is quite important to realize that unlike the shepherd metaphor, the king-host metaphor is oft oblivious or utterly omitted in the Poem. Many scholarly writings, Philip Nel J. points out, focus mainly on the "metaphorical expressions involving the shepherd and associated with God—hence . . . God is [seen as] a shepherd."[4]

---

[2] Hermann Gunkel, *The Psalms: A Form-Critical Introduction,* trans. Thomas M. Horner (Tubingen: Fortress Press, 1967), 10.

[3] Gottfried Voigt, "The Speaking Christ in His Royal Office." *Concordia Theological Monthly 23* (1952): 161–75.

[4] Philip Nel J., "Yahweh Is a Shepherd: Conceptual Metaphor in Psalm 23." *Horizons in Biblical Theology 27* (2005): 79–103.

Erwin Blasa and Clarence Marquez explain that some are satisfied with "the figure of Jesus Christ as the Shepherd of the church . . . [and still, others] propose a possible application of the sheep-and-shepherd image in Psalm 23."[5]

It should also be noted that the purpose of this book is not to negate the shepherd interpretation as the Psalm, indeed, includes shepherd imaginings.

The direction of this manuscript is to offer furtherance of thought to the already satiated mind in pointing out the deliberate royal language inscribed in the Psalm. My motivation for this writing stems from my own experience with Christ as my Lord and King, and the belief that David intended for the shepherd metaphor to be recognized as a counterpart to the king-host metaphor, which he introduces later in the Psalm, establishing a complete image of how he sees YHWH.

The Lord lends tender care to His children like a shepherd unto his sheep, and yet, He reigns supreme over the flock as the One who has final authority over its well-being and destiny.

My approach to Psalm 23 for this book is more exegetical and expository, encompassing its metaphors' historical, cultural, and modern contexts while demonstrating the author's intentional paradigm shift from shepherd metaphor to royal imagery inscribed in the Psalm.

---

[5] Erwin Blasa and Clarence Marquez, "Towards A 'Shepherd' Spirituality: The Application of the Image of Sheep-and-Shepherd in Psalm 23 to Seminary Formation in the Philippines." *Philippiniana Sacra 45*, no. 135 (September 2010): 610–70.

Shepherding played a central role in the lives of the Israelites as a pastoral society.

SECTION ONE

CHAPTER ONE—THE SHEPHERD METAPHOR

From the superscription of Psalm 23, Davidic authorship is made explicit. It is a well-known fact that David himself was shepherd and king. His experience with taking care of people and sheep afforded him a more extensive understanding of a shepherd's duty.

Nonetheless, Jacqulyn Thorpe Brown lets us understand that, here "in the 23rd Psalm, David is not speaking as the shepherd, although he was one, but as a sheep—as one of the flock."[6] Hence, more than an explication of YHWH, the Psalm is an experience with YHWH.

He begins the Psalm with an exclamation:

"The Lord is my Shepherd." (v. 1a)

This declaration becomes the engine on which the remainder of the Psalm runs. All other statements that follow, will be in relation to who the Shepherd is.

---

[6] Jacqulyn Thorpe Brown, "Psalm 23: A Remix." *Journal of Religious Thought 59/60,* no. 1/2, 1 (January 2006): 165–79.

Hope, trust, expectation, and exultation are only possible when the Shepherd has proven trustworthy. As the sheep becomes more and more acquainted with such a shepherd, it will naturally express confidence in that shepherd.

Hence, the potency of the Psalm becomes contingent upon the Shepherd's competency.

The author uses the word *shepherd* to describe YHWH. Why shepherd?

According to the narratives of the OT, shepherding played a central role in the lives of the Israelites as a pastoral society. Abraham, Moses, David, and Amos, the prophet, were all shepherds. The annual shearing in Israel was an event worthy of royal attention. (2 Sam. 13:23ff) Genesis 47:3 records the answer of the sons of Jacob to the questioning of Pharaoh concerning their occupation: "Your servants are shepherds."

Shepherding was looked upon favorably since the fat-portioned offering of Abel, the herdsman, was received by YHWH. In contrast, YHWH rejected the crops offering of his brother Cain.

As the ancient reader read Psalm 23, he imagined the shepherd as tending sheep and leading his people. Jørn Varhug observes that when St. Jerome translated Psalm 23:1 with "Dominus Regit me,"—*the Lord rules me*, he was probably closer to the first reading than when he later renders it "Dominus pascit me," meaning *the Lord pastures me*, though *pascit* is a more direct translation from the Hebrew רֹעִי *(to pasture)*.[7]

In other terms, the implication of being a "shepherd" is greater than its definition—who the shepherd is, exceeds what the shepherd does. His reputation precedes Him, and His character is the basis for his reputation.

---

[7]   Jørn Varhaug, "The Decline of the Shepherd Metaphor as Royal Self-Expression1." *SJOT: Scandinavian Journal of the Old Testament 33,* no. 1 (May 2019): 16–23.

YHWH is all-knowing and all-powerful. He could abuse His power, and mistreat His sheep if He wanted to, and there would be no other power strong enough to contend with Him.

However, He does not abuse His power to mistreat His sheep because that is simply not Who He is.

In the ancient Near East, society used the shepherd role and title to depict their relationship to the people in their charge. Metaphorically, "shepherd" increasingly acquired a specific royal connotation, especially in the pre-exilic era.

"Gods and kings were labeled the shepherd of their people. Both described and portrayed with mace (rod) and shepherd's crook (staff) as regalia of office."[8] (I will further elaborate on that in verse four). Even Ezekiel and Isaiah depict the image of YHWH as "the strong One," and "like a shepherd," referring to His kingship (Ez. 34; Is. 40: 9-11).[9]

Even in modern society, the term "shepherd" describes leadership positions, such as kings, pastors, teachers, and the like, though it is used more exclusively for pastors.

In Spanish, *shepherd* translates into "*pastor.*"

Many of my congregants call me "shepherd." The ones who call me shepherd imply that they recognize me as the one in their charge, after God. Hence, it is evident that the shepherd governs the sheep. However, how the shepherd rules over the sheep determines failure or success and the kind of shepherd he is.

---

[8]   James Mayes Luther, *Psalms-Interpretation-A Bible Commentary for Teaching and Preaching* (Louisville: John Knox Press, [1994]), 117.

[9]   Daniel Muthunayagom Jones. "The Image of God as King and the Nature of His Power in the Old Testament." *Bangalore Theological Forum 41*, no. 2 (2009): 29–48.

PRAYING IN PSALM 23

Prayer #1

Yahweh is my Shepherd,

Thus, all my needs are met;

Yahweh is my Shepherd,

Henceforth, I shall not fret.

NOTES

_____

_____

_____

_____

_____

_____

_____

_____

_____

_____

CHAPTER TWO—THE POSITION OF THE SHEPHERD

I concluded the previous chapter with the notion that the shepherd rules over the sheep. The shepherd metaphor in Psalm 23, however, denotes more than YHWH ruling over His creation. The allegory rather implies an authoritative figure who is also capable of providing personal and tender care. From the outset, David acknowledges YHWH as is his Shepherd denoting that He is the One who takes care of him, the One who possesses the satisfaction and the provision in attending to his needs.

The shepherd imagery, Dr. Martin Klingbeil notes, is one "that runs through the Bible as a beautiful image of God's care and provision with messianic overtone."[10] Jesus confirms that view in John 10:11 when He says: "I am the good Shepherd, and the good Shepherd gives His life for His sheep." A mercenary leaves the sheep unattended, but the good Shepherd gives His life for the sheep. Having had such a clear understanding of the kind of shepherd YHWH is, David expresses utter confidence in the Lord as his Shepherd, the One on Whom he ought to rely even in the direst situation.

Having claimed YHWH as his Shepherd, David begins to express his profusion as well as his expectation of Him, in saying:

---

[10]   Martin Klingbeil G., "Psalm 23." *Seventh-day Adventist International Bible Commentary* [in print].

"I shall not want." (v. 1b)

The Hebrew word translated into "want" is אֶחְסָר: *(echsar)*, which means lacking, decrease, deprive, or do without.

However, a more sensible translation would be *I lack nothing,* or *I have no lack;* as David Clines points out, "plainly the focus of vv. 1-5 is on the speaker's experience, in the present."[11] Nevertheless, given that the verb is in its imperfect form, a translation in the future tense can be justified.

The usage of such language in the text suggests that David was indeed experiencing a sense of present satisfaction in retrospect of his past dealings with YHWH, which gave him the confidence of assuming a secured future in Him.

As David basks in *grateful living,* the present is no longer being lived in consternation, but rather in conviction, out of contemplation of past conditions. And because YHWH has proven Himself faithful in the past, He can be trusted for the future. The statement "I shall not want," then, becomes a fluid concept which travels from the past through the present and unto the future, with the assurance that come what may, one ought not to fret for YHWH shall remain ever faithful.

My Personal Experience with YHWH

The year was 2010, and I set out on a venture that would change my life forever. I was the Founder and CEO of a Christian promotion company called Leap of Faith Entertainment (LFE), and I planned to produce the biggest Christian concert of the year in my community.

---

[11] David Clines J. A., "The Lord Is My Shepherd in East and South East Asia." *Sino-Christian Studies* (June 2006): 37–54.

The plans were made, and the date was set. It would be on October 10, 2010, hence the slogan, "**10.10.10.**"

We wanted to host the cream of the crop, la crème de la crème of local artists, with the addition of a One-Hundred-Voice African Choir which would come from out of town. The expenses were enormous.

Because LFE was at its incipiency, we acquired very few financial endorsements. We relied extensively on local churches to finance this mega-concert. Fast forward two weeks before the program, the churches we relied on the most fell through—they returned entire stacks of tickets to us in pristine condition.

Not one sold!

I immediately fell into despair. I was in such a state of depression that once, after getting up from my bed, I involuntarily fell flat backward on the bed. It was then, I looked up to the ceiling in desperation and spoke to YHWH: "Lord!" I implored, "if You allow this concert to be a success, I will no longer doubt You about anything else in my life." Instantaneously, I recovered my strength and went about my way.

With much gratitude, I am delighted to testify to you that "**10.10.10**" was one of the most significant accomplishments of my life. We had a sold-out concert with more than 2500 attendees, and the VIP section costing $100 per person, sold out first. Though the show was costly, we generated enough revenue from ticket sales to come out of this endeavor debt-free!

Based on that experience, whenever the time comes for me to doubt my faith in God, I doubt my doubts instead and keep believing what I believe.

Like David, because of my personal experience with YHWH, even now, I can exclaim amid my trials, "I shall not want!" Thus, because my Shepherd has proven Himself trustworthy in the past, I trust Him for the future.

It is beneficial to comprehend that David is not referring merely to material riches in saying "I shall not want" or "I lack nothing." On the contrary, I believe David intended to point out that many blessings which YHWH bestows on those He shepherds are not necessarily tangible riches. These benefits transcend concrete domains, and they manifest themselves exclusively through the presence of the Lord.

It goes without saying that "this Shepherd attends to both the physical needs of the sheep and to the soul."[12]

As an Israelite youth who went through the ritual of Bar Mitzvah, assuredly David was taught from the chronicles of his ancestors how for forty years YHWH cared for them, and they "lacked nothing." (Deut. 2:7) I imagine David was also taught about his forefathers looking forward to the Promised Land in which God foretold that they "will lack nothing." (Deut. 8:9)

Early on, David clearly understood that the shepherd was also the provider. In his day, it was equally acknowledged that the king who held the scepter as insignia of royalty assumed the responsibility to protect and provide for the people. Consequently, David is saying because the Lord is his Shepherd, he shall not lack anything he needs.

---

[12]   Dianne Bergant, *Psalms 1-72*, vol. 22. *New Collegeville Bible Commentary, Old Testament,* (Collegeville, Minnesota: Liturgical Press, [2013]), 21.

It is imperative to realize that claiming YHWH as one's Shepherd is not an exclusive concept to David alone. A shepherd-sheep relationship is available to WHOSOEVER desires to pursue a connection with the Lord.

Whatever your nationality, ethnicity, legal or social status, your current religious belief, or the lack thereof, you are eligible for a covenant relationship with the Lord.

Galatians 3:26-29 says:

> "For you are all sons of God through faith in Christ Jesus.
> For as many of you as were baptized into Christ have put on Christ.
> There is neither Jew nor Greek, there is neither slave nor free,
> there is neither male nor female; for you are all one in Christ Jesus.
> And if you are Christ's, then you are Abraham's seed,
> and heirs according to the promise."

Furthermore, Jesus, the good Shepherd, promised in John 6:37: "All that the Father gives Me will come to Me, and the one who comes to Me I will by no means cast out." Thus, all those who trust in YHWH, like David, may confidently claim the Lord as their Shepherd.

PRAYING IN PSALM 23

Prayer #2

Yahweh is my Shepherd,

My Load has been carried.

Yahweh is my Shepherd,

Hence, I am not worried.

NOTES

He makes me to lie in green pastures; He leads me besides the still waters.

14

CHAPTER THREE—THE LEADERSHIP OF THE SHEPHERD

eing a poet, David uses aesthetic language and imagery, pointing to key locations and other props to evoke crucial theological perceptions of the shepherd's leadership.

"He makes me to lie in green pastures; He leads me besides the still waters." (v. 2)

Here, David is emphasizing the Lord's grace and guidance as the ultimate basis for goodness. YHWH leads the flock to green pastures for grazing and resting while ruminating, and then down to calm potable water to quench their thirst.

In a more profound sense, *green pastures* indicate provision and prosperity, while *still waters* point to a peaceful state. As God provides for our every need, He also ensures our peace of mind. No more do we need to become anxious by the cares of this life, for Jehovah Jireh fulfills our wants and, in so doing, eliminates our worries.

The guidance of the Lord goes beyond providence to morality. In providing the best for the flock, the Shepherd leads them to decency and dignity. They have every good reason to trust in His leadership. Whereas earthly shepherds may lead their sheep astray, the divine caring Shepherd will only lead His herd to incredible vistas where they will find physical sustenance, rest, and peace of mind.

How excellent of a Shepherd is YHWH! What a kind and thoughtful Ruler is He! Is He not worthy to be praised? Is He not worthy to be worshipped and adored?

Not only He cares about our physical and spiritual state, but He also cares about our mental state. Our dignity matters to Him; our peace of mind is of top interest to Him. For this reason, He will make a way where there seems to be no way for all who choose to be under His care.

Hallelujah! To Him be all the honor and all the glory!

"He restores my soul." (v. 3a)

The Hebrew word for restore derives from the verb root שׁוּב *(shoov)* which means to bring back to the ideal condition.

Some scholars date Psalm 23 back to when King Saul was persecuting David. That period would have been a moment of great distress for David. The nefarious pursuit of Saul would surely bring trouble to David's soul rendering him exhausted and depleted, and as YHWH led him to places where he could eat, drink, and rest, he renewed his strength, and he was invigorated to move forward.

In this context, one may conclude that God's leadership has proven to be salvific in that He restored his life to an even better state than before. Thus, David acknowledges that when his soul was in peril, Jehovah was the One who restored him to the ideal condition.

The Hope of Restoration for Today

Living in our world today, one cannot be oblivious to the discouragement and despair caused by the vicissitudes of life and the precariousness of our time.

Who can forget the worldwide turmoil our world experienced in 2020, which bled even into 2021?

Who, regardless of political stance, is not puzzled or bewildered at the sight of complete mayhem caused by riots and political unrests throughout the Land of the Free and elsewhere?

Who is not crying out for God's mercy when viewing all the global disaster videos on social media occurring daily?

Who is not alarmed by the outcome of the deadly plague of COVID-19, which seems to have eradicated life's normalcy?

So many restrictions—the closing of churches, restaurants, and favorite places of leisure; so many losses—unprecedented fatalities; entire families swept away—many are left financially bankrupt, and perhaps, facing eviction from their home; many are left orphans, widows, and widowers; and scientists are predicting so much more to come.

Each of these events mentioned above is enough to cause panic; unfortunately, many are affected by their combination.

Perhaps, you or others you know have been personally affected in more ways than one, and it feels like you are broken into a thousand unmendable pieces.

Despite the pain you might be experiencing, it would be quite beneficial to remember that restoration is still available today to those whose Shepherd is YHWH. Is YHWH your Shepherd? Are you in need of restoration?

Trusting in Him is an appropriate start toward your complete restoration.

Why not begin today?

NOTES

When YHWH,
the Shepherd, is leading,
even when the paths of
righteousness do not look
right in the eyes of the sheep,
they will Always lead to the
intended destination.

CHAPTER FOUR—THE CHARACTER OF THE SHEPHERD

"He leads me in the paths of righteousness." (v. 3b)

The original Hebrew word צֶדֶק *(tseh'-dek)* translated into *righteousness* evokes a sense of what is ethically right, leading to a perfect end. A better translation vis-à-vis sheep would be "right paths."

Right paths, Clines observes, "can only be the paths that are right in the shepherd's judgment as best for the sheep. And that must mean: paths that lead to food and water even if they run through a dark valley (v.4)."[13]

The character of the shepherd is at play here. A shepherd that leads his sheep to food, water, and rest is a good shepherd.

YHWH leads in the paths of righteousness because He is righteous. His righteous deeds are not derived from His position, but from His own righteousness.

---

[13] David Clines J. A., "The Lord Is My Shepherd in East and South East Asia." *Sino-Christian Studies* (June 2006): 37–54.

When YHWH, the Shepherd, is leading, even when the *paths of righteousness* do not look right in the eyes of the sheep, they will ALWAYS lead to the intended destination. God's ways are accurate because of His perfect character. There is no repercussion for the benefits the sheep enjoy because they come from a pure and honorable source.

"For His name's sake." (v. 3c)

Sheep are not the most intelligent animals. Sometimes they choose to go the wrong way despite the directive effort of the shepherd. He still goes after the strayed sheep to bring them back to the fold.

The actions of the shepherd are not contingent upon the merit of the sheep. As David Adamo puts it, "Yahweh decides to protect His people, 'for His name sake,' that is, His nature, His holy character, is power and all that Yahweh is."[14]

That explains why "He makes His sun rise on the evil and on the good and sends rain on the just and on the unjust." (Matt 5:45)

Even those who do not acknowledge YHWH as their Shepherd are blessed by Him, nonetheless.

The one who curses YHWH, as he breathes the words out of his mouth, is using the very air that God created to do so.

The one who rejects YHWH is still loved by Him.

---

[14] David Adamo T., "Reading Psalm 23 in African Context." *Verbum et Ecclesia 39*, no. 1 (January 2018): 1–8.

God is concerned
with the sheep
that remain in the
sheepfold as He is
with the lost ones.

The Black Sheep
are marginalized–the
odd ones in the group.

His love for ALL his sheep does not fluctuate and He has mercy on the flock not just to protect His reputation, as some may assume, but because He is being consistent with His own character.

God is concerned with the sheep that remain in the sheepfold as He is with the lost ones; and He guards the flock impartially from predators and dangers of any kind.[15]

Prophet Isaiah made a statement apropos the sheep going astray: "All we like sheep," the Prophet says, "have gone astray; we have turned everyone to his own way, and the Lord has laid on Him the iniquity of us all." (Is. 53:6) Such is YHWH, and that is the kind of God we serve.

Do you feel like a lost sheep? God is concerned about you.

When Isaiah says: "All we like sheep have gone astray," it means that *we are all like sheep.* One's agreement or disagreement with this argument does not lessen its veracity. We did not create ourselves and are in constant need to be led, cared for, and protected, making us all "like sheep," for we are in the same condition as they are.

We all belong to one of the following classifications of sheep: Lost Sheep, Black Sheep, or Safe Sheep.

The Lost Sheep. This category contains the sheep that have wandered away from the flock for whatever reason and cannot find their way. Whether those sheep wander out of their own volition or by influence or ignorance, they still need to be rescued.

---

[15]   Dianne Bergant, *Psalms 1-72*, vol. 22. *New Collegeville Bible Commentary, Old Testament,* (Collegeville, Minnesota: Liturgical Press, [2013]), 21.

The Black Sheep. This kind is marginalized—the odd ones in the group. The term *black sheep* stems from the black color of a sheep's fleece, which cannot dye like the others that are more common white, and therefore, considered less valuable. This type of sheep is looked upon less favorably and is less likable. It is esteemed of less worth than others, and it may be targeted unfairly by another (one of the same fold or another domain). They, too, need to be defended.

Then, there is the **Safe Sheep.** This category of sheep contains the ones that follow the shepherd's guidance and accomplish all they need for their well-being. Those sheep, also, are sustained by the continual guidance, protection, and provision of the shepherd to maintain the "safe" lifestyle.

The lost sheep need to be rescued, the black sheep need to be defended, and the safe sheep must be sustained.

Hence, do you see the point of the argument? Is that not all of us? Are we not all in need of being rescued, defended, and sustained by YHWH?

Thanks be to God! He is not partial in His dealings with us, nor is He incapable of producing anything we lack.

Not only He has strength, but He also possesses absolute power to change the course of events that He may accomplish all His desires on our behalf.

He is concerned about all of us, whether we be lost sheep, black sheep, or safe sheep.

To Him be all the glory!!!

PRAYING IN PSALM 23

Prayer #3

Yahweh is my Shepherd,

He is my Hope and Stay;

Yahweh is my Shepherd,

He leads me all the way.

NOTES

The mere presence of the shepherd keeps the vicious foes away from the sheep.

CHAPTER FIVE—THE PRESENCE OF THE SHEPHERD

Sheep are meek and mild, docile, and even dumb. Often, ferocious animals, such as wolves, seek to prey on their vulnerability. The mere presence of the shepherd keeps the vicious foes away from the sheep. Thus, the presence of the shepherd is very significant to the sheep.

The shepherd speaks to the sheep as he leads them on their way. They know his voice, and he knows theirs. Hearing the shepherd's voice, the sheep realize which way to go while the attackers see that it is not proper to attack. The sheer presence of the shepherd becomes the safety net of the flock.

The assertiveness of the shepherd, which enables him to know when the sheep are hungry, tired, or hurt, brings them comfort. The sheep unquestionably recognize the difference between the presence and the absence of the shepherd.

"Yea, though I walk through the valley of the shadow of death." (v. 4a)

Some scholars believe that the valley of the shadow of death did exist. Whether it did or not, Gerald Wilson observes that "there is some evidence that in Hebrew for the use of

Hyperbolic word constructions such as this one to experience the superlative, the most extreme."[16]

A valley is already a low place, then shadow expresses darkness, and death is the ultimate place of darkness. David presents this poetic imagery to point out the apex of any dreadful condition.

Simply put, any situation that could end in death without the shepherd's intervention is a "valley of the shadow of death" because, in such a situation, death could be seen or even felt in the shadows.

This dreadful condition described as the "shadow of death" can also be created by a blockage from the shepherd's presence. Shadows evoke the spaces formed when an object obstructs the pathway of light. When any given object blocks the presence of the shepherd representing the light, darkness prevails.

YHWH cannot be seen by those He shepherds because He is Spirit, and they are matter. However, He does not have to be seen for His presence to be felt. He is seen through the manifestation of His presence. Yet, His appearance can be manifested, but not perceived by the sheep, if the sheep are submerged in sin.

Since sin is a producer of deception, division, and desolation, one can say that sin is the ultimate cause of the sheep plunging into the *shadow of death,* away from the sustenance of the Shepherd's presence.

---

[16]   Gerald Wilson H., *The NIV Application Commentary, Psalm* vol. 1, (Grand Rapids, MI: Zondervan, [2002]), 434.

Never did he take his flock where he had not already been before. Always he had gone ahead to look over the country with care.

Using this hyperbolic language, David is stressing that his confidence is in knowing that the Lord abides with him always. David is essentially saying no matter how awful or dark the situation may appear, from the matrix of his experience with YHWH, his trust will not waver, because YHWH, as his Shepherd, will not lead him to a place where He had not been Himself.

That notion is echoed in Psalm 139: 7-10:

> Where can I go from Your Spirit?
> Or where can I flee from Your presence?
> If I ascend into heaven, You are there;
> If I make my bed in hell, behold, You are there.
> If I take the wings of the morning,
> And dwell in the uttermost parts of the sea,
> Even there Your hand shall lead me,
> And Your right hand shall hold me.

As a shepherd, David knew firsthand the difficulties, the dangers, and the delights of the treks into the elevated countryside.

"Never did he take his flock where he had not already been before. Always he had gone ahead to look over the country with care."[17]

Having such knowledge about shepherding, the Psalmist builds his confidence in the Lord as his Shepherd; and consequently, he feels safe even when going through the valley of the shadow of death.

---

[17]   Phillip Keller W., *A Shepherd's Look At Psalm 23*, (Grand Rapids, MI: Zondervan Publishing House, 1970-71), 83.

The Presence of the Shepherd Produces Confidence—Trust in the Sheep

"I will fear no evil." (v. 4b)

Those two words: fear יָרֵא *(yare)* and evil רָע *(ra)* are worth pausing over.

Fear (יָרֵא), in its various forms, appears in 331 occurrences in the OT. It means an unpleasant, sometimes strong emotion caused by awareness or anticipation of danger. Fear is often marked by a past event or anxiety of the unknown.

Thus, we may define "fear" as *a lack of confidence in future outcome* based on past experiences; and "confidence in future outcome," *hope;* and "hope," *the antidote for fear*—especially hope in YHWH, for He is Omniscient knowing the future from the beginning.

In war or a duel, fearmongering may be a prevalent tactic used to torment the enemy as fear may cause ominous moods through anxiety, depression, discouragement, stagnation, leading to downright defeat. For this reason, YHWH is constantly warning His people against fear.

Evil (רָע) on the other hand, is distress, misery, calamity, injury, or anything that causes unpleasant situations. Evil and fear walk hand in hand, and evil of any kind may be an effective weapon to inflict fear. Yet, David declares: "I will fear no evil," demonstrating ultimate confidence and utter dependence on YHWH. Only a close relationship with the Lord may result in such faith in the face of evil.

We Will Fear
No Evil!

This calls to mind the story of King Jehoshaphat, who, in the face of menacing evil from conspiring neighboring countries, expressed similar confidence in YHWH as he prayed: "O our God...we know not what to do, but our eyes *are* upon You." (2 Chro. 20:12) Here, "our eyes are upon You" really means *our hope is in You.* Such is the level of confidence in God that will cast out all fear.

The Presence of the Shepherd is Protection—Peace of Mind for the Sheep

"For You *are* with me." (v. 4c)

The presence of the shepherd represents protection for the sheep. And here, once more, David is expressing the Lord's blessing in the form of His presence as a protective instrument.

His conviction derives from the covenant between YHWH and Israel, and, as Michael Goulder points out, also from "the promise that God will be with them is a standard expression of that covenant, coupled with a charge not to fear."[18]

The presence of God has been explicit in Scripture as the reason why the Israelites had not any reason to be afraid. To Jacob YHWH said: "Behold, I *am* with you and will keep you wherever you go." (Gen. 28:15) To the children of Israel, He declared: "The past forty years, the Lord has been with you;" (Deut. 2:7) "Do not be afraid of them; for the Lord your God *is* with you;" (Deut. 20:1) "Fear not, for I *am* with you." (Is. 41:10) Over and over again, Israel's protection is expressed to be contingent upon God's presence. David also believes that his own deliverance in danger rests solely in the presence of YHWH.

A friend of mine from Malawi, East Africa, a contemporary of my wife, explains how he used to be afraid of the dark when he was growing up. The somber and gloomy feeling of the

---

18   Michael Goulder, "David and Yahweh in Psalms 23 and 24." *Journal for the Study of the Old Testament 30,* no. 4 (June 2006): 463–73.

dark of night terrified him. However, once someone else held his hand, he felt safe though he could not see them physically.

This scenario further explains that what my friend fears more than the dark is **being alone** in the dark. For once he experiences the presence of someone else with him, the dread of the night goes away.

God the Father, wanting to reassure today's believers that He is still with us, names His only begotten Son "Emmanuel"—God with us. (Is. 7:14; Matt. 1:23) It is that same presence that compels the Apostle Paul to pose the question, "If God be for us, who can be against us?"(εἰ ὁ Θεὸς ὑπὲρ ἡμῶν τίς καθ᾽ ἡμῶν? Rom. 8:31). The preposition ὑπὲρ (hoo.per), in the Greek, means: over; beyond; on behalf of; for the sake of; or concerning. It is usually best translated *for the betterment or the advantage of,* or *having a sense of interest in.* However, it can also mean, *in the place of* or *instead of.*

In essence, the notion that God is with us goes beyond Him being above watching over us; He is actually with us, and, for our betterment, He is ready to act in our stead in times of trouble.

March 19, 2008

I used to be a Limo Driver. I mainly drove locally in the tri-county metropolitan area of south Florida. However, one time, I had to transport a vehicle from Indiana back to South Florida.

My then boss and I flew to Indiana, and on the same day, we picked up the vehicles we were to drive respectively, back down south. He drove a ten pax limo while I drove a Ford Expedition SUV. He went ahead, and I followed. We slept some on the side of the road, but we drove most of the night and continued on the next day.

In the middle of the afternoon, while passing an area near the University of Florida (UF) in Gainesville, suddenly I heard a big bang. All I remember was my vehicle veering off the road and headed to the trees in the forest. Being in shock from the trauma, all I kept uttering was: "O! God. O! God. O! God." At that point, I thought to myself: "This is it! I will surely go to my grave today."

In the meantime, the car kept flipping as I kept crying to the Lord. Finally, the vehicle struck a tree, and it stopped.

To my great astonishment, I came out of the vehicle with just a lump on my head from hitting it on the car ceiling.

While the car was a total loss, I was totally safe. Why?

Because YHWH, My Shepherd, was with me. His mighty hands gripped mine, and the Protective Shepherd successfully carried me out to safety.

I later found out that a young student looking for the university saw that she was about to lose the exit, and she quickly switched lanes without paying much attention to my car next to hers. She hit the rear fender of the vehicle by accident, and the fender locked on the back wheel of the Expedition, which rendered it unmanageable.

The way the accident happened, it should have been the end of me! I should have walked through the valley of the shadow of death, never to return to this side of history. But God had a better plan for my life.

March 19, 2008, which could have been the end of my journey here on earth, became a Memorial Day for when YHWH walked with me *through the valley of the shadow of death* and brought me out unscathed.

Even when it doesn't seem like it, YHWH is with us!

For this reason, even when the tumultuous storms of life seem to be rising above us as when ferocious wolves tower over vulnerable sheep, like David, we may exclaim:

"WE WILL FEAR NO EVIL!"

For I am persuaded that the presence of God that protected David has the same protective power today.

PRAYING IN PSALM 23

Prayer #4

Yahweh is my Shepherd,

So, I am not alone;

Yahweh is my Shepherd,

And that is set in stone!

NOTES

Ancient iconographies such as emblems and monuments portrayed kings like Pharaoh holding the flail and staff.

SECTION TWO

CHAPTER SIX—A PARADIGM SHIFT

"Your rod and Your staff, they comfort me." (v. 4c)

T he psalmist mentions both the rod שֵׁבֶט (*shevet*) and the staff מִשְׁעֶנֶת (*mishenet*). The Bible uses these two words interchangeably.

In this instance, however, I believe the author is making a segue from the *Shepherd* view to the *King-Host* view. The wordplay serves as a conduit to transmit the reader's mind from pastoral care to royal treatment.

In Chapter One, we saw that in the ancient Near East, kings were considered the shepherds, protectors, and judges of their people. In connection to that notion, ancient iconographies such as emblems and monuments portrayed kings like Pharaoh holding the flail and staff.

According to Leviticus 27:32, the Hebrew word *shevet* describes a shepherd's rod, whereas in Numbers 21:18 *mishenet* refers to staves of princes and rulers. Your rod and your staff, (שֵׁבֶט, מִשְׁעֶנֶת), are viewed as comforting instruments of protection and direction, respectively.

This section of the Psalm conveys the correlation between shepherd and king best. The argument evoking that the vocation of the king is to protect, guide, and care for the people even at the expense of his own life becomes more plausible.[19] In retrospect, a shepherd

---

[19]   David Adamo T., "Reading Psalm 23 in African Context." *Verbum et Ecclesia 39*, no. 1 (January 2018): 1–8.

plays both roles as the one taking tender loving care of the sheep and the one ruling over or leading the sheep. He is the able Protector and the abundant Provider. Hence, the Lord is simultaneously the Shepherd and the King-Host.

The Banquet Imagery

To ensure that his readers grasp this paradigm shift, David presents the following statement as a clutch:

"You prepare a table before me in the presence of my enemies." (v. 5a)

The author now shifts to the second image of YHWH, who hosts a lavish banquet for him as His guest of honor. The strict code of hospitality in the Near East obliged hosts to offer their best meals for guests, including those who might be enemies. The Psalmist is now describing a banquet of honor that goes beyond nourishment to a public witness of YHWH's high regard for him.[20]

---

[20] Dianne Bergant, *Psalms 1-72*, vol. 22. *New Collegeville Bible Commentary, Old Testament*, (Collegeville, Minnesota: Liturgical Press, [2013]), 22.

As a Shepherd, the Lord leads to green pastures and beside still waters, but as a King-Host, the Lord prepares a table to receive His guests.

It is striking to see how the imagery has progressed.

As a Shepherd, the Lord leads to green pastures and beside still waters, but as a King-Host, the Lord prepares a table to receive His guests. A shepherd does not set tables, a king does.

From my visits to excavation sites in Israel, one distinct feature that distinguished the kings' palaces from commoners' abodes, were the long dining halls. The kings had many feasts, and it was a customary practice for them to invite common people on special occasions to dine with the dignitaries, especially if they wanted to appease the people and veered them from an uproar.

A day before the feast, the peasant's treatment was far inferior to that of the noble; however, everyone is honored equally at the king's table. The lord could fiercely despise the commoner, but they were all eating at the same table on that day. Royal Court officials who might have also been rivals had no choice but to be amicable in the presence of the king.

Ps. 113:7-8 reverberates the idea of YHWH setting up a table to honor those who might otherwise be despised in saying:

> "He raises the poor from the dust,
> And lifts the needy from the ash heap,
> To make them sit with princes,
> With the princes of his people."

I am a living witness to such a reality. Perhaps you, too, may attest to the truthfulness of this text, based on your own experience with the Lord. God is good!

The mention of "my enemies" in the text is an indication that the feast offered by YHWH is more telling than at first look. Goulder observes that "the word צֹרֵר [(Tsarar) for enemy] is found in a military context (Num. 10:9; Is. 11:13) and would be well suited to a king."[21] It suggests a sense of vindication.

"The reason," Ron Tappy notes, "is that those enemies who taunt and provoke or vex the sheep of YHWH actually intend to challenge and defy the power of YHWH Himself to defend them."[22]

As stated in Psalm 89:50-51, the righteous suffer the reproach of YHWH's enemies. And those taunts usually imply the rhetorical questions, where is their God? Can He or will He come to their aid?

Consequently, the King-Host, in the same manner, the Shepherd provided green pastures and still waters for the sheep, now provides a table and a cup as sustenance and a safe haven to his guest of honor. It is worth noticing that both metaphors are underlying *food* and *drink*, which further strengthen their parallel connection.

Furthermore, the meal or feast in the Psalm is a plausible representation of the sealing of a covenant relationship between the guest and the host, as eating and drinking was the capstone event that sealed covenant relationships in ancient times. (see Exodus 24) Jesus also mentioned a lavish feast at the return of the Prodigal Son to seal the patrimonial covenant relationship between father and son as he gained back his sonship. (Luke 15:22)

David may be demonstrating a deeper level of relationship that leads to God, as the Host, eventually adopting him—the guest, as kinsmen, which would entitle him to stay in the house and even socioeconomic benefits.

---

21 Michael Goulder, "David and Yahweh in Psalms 23 and 24." *Journal for the Study of the Old Testament 30*, no. 4 (June 2006): 463–73.

22 Ron Tappy E, "Psalm 23: Symbolism and Structure." *The Catholic Biblical Quarterly 57*, no. 2 (April 1995): 255–80.

PRAYING IN PSALM 23

Prayer #5

Yahweh is my Shepherd,

He shall conquer my foe;

Yahweh is my Shepherd,

He's my Superhero!

NOTES

Anointment was thought to endow a prince with divine blessing and some degree of priestly (possibly even divine) character.

- 52 -

CHAPTER SEVEN—THE ANOINTING OF OIL IMAGERY

"You anoint my head with oil." (v. 5b)

The biblical imagery of anointing is frequently associated with blessings. (Ps. 45:7; Eccles. 9:8; Amos 6:6; Luke 7:46) Elsewhere in the Psalms of Ascents, David juxtaposes the anointing of oil once again with God's blessings. In Psalm 133:1-3, he writes:

Behold, how good and how pleasant *it is*
For brethren to dwell together in unity!
It is like the **precious oil upon the head,**
Running down on the beard,
The beard of Aaron,
Running down on the edge of his garments.
It is like the dew of Hermon,
Descending upon the mountains of Zion;
For there the LORD commanded the **blessing—**
Life forevermore.

By now, David has had firsthand experience with being anointed with oil. Spooling back to the genesis of David's story, it comes to mind when upon the insistence of the people, Samuel reluctantly anointed Saul, who had a king's height but not a king's heart.

Eventually, God rejected him and sent Samuel to Bethlehem in search of a new king, except this time the king will not be chosen by humans but by God who "looks at the heart." (1 Sam. 16:7)

Jesse's seven eldest sons passed before Samuel without a "hit." David, the eighth and youngest son, was summoned, and this time the Lord said to Samuel: "Rise and anoint him; for this is the one." (1 Sam. 16:12) Samuel obeys and anoints David's head with oil, and as Marti Steussy explains, "and the Spirit of the Lord came mightily upon David from that day forward."[23]

According to *Columbia Electronic Encyclopedia,* the anointing of David was more than ordinary blessings "because anointment was thought to endow a prince with divine blessing and some degree of priestly (possibly even divine) character."[24] It is safe to say that the statement "you anoint my head with oil" is possibly stemmed from the many blessings that God had been bestowing on David up until then through a series of well-documented events in the Bible, such as his victory against Goliath which gained him national heroic recognition.

In addition to blessings, oil imagery can also be associated with healing. Sheep are well-known for their docile and inane ways which sometimes afford them to obliviously hurt their head going through the caves or against tight ways. The shepherd would subsequently anoint the head of the sheep to soothe and heal the pain.

Even today, we still anoint the sick with oil. As a pastor, I anoint my sick members who request the anointing of oil for their sickness. "Is anyone among you sick?" The Apostle James asks, "let him call for the elders of the church, and let them pray over him, anointing him with oil in the name of the Lord." (James 5:14)

---

[23] Marti Steussy J, *David : Biblical Portraits of Power. Studies on Personalities of the Old Testament.* (Columbia, S.C.: University of South Carolina Press, 1999), 41-42.

[24] Coronation." *Columbia Electronic Encyclopedia,* 6th ed., (February 2020), 1.

When a sheep goes its own way and gets injured, more than the physical healing, the sheep needs restoration.

Hence, in addition to the shepherd leading and providing for the lamb, he also healed the lamb.

It is worth pointing out that YHWH's healing power is connected to the seven-fold notion of **love**, **mercy**, **grace**, **forgiveness**, **salvation**, **hope**, and **restoration**. For when YHWH heals, He makes whole. He forgives, He gives hope, and He restores. No ill escapes His diagnosis; His stethoscope picks up the slightest irregularity from the heartbeat. For whatever type of healing is needed, whether physical, mental, or spiritual, Jehovah Rapha has the remedy.

Daniel O'Kennedy clarifies that "healing is more than medically verifiable physical restoration; it includes a deeper dimension of forgiveness and restoration into the fellowship with God."[25]

When a sheep goes its own way and gets injured, more than the physical healing, the sheep needs restoration. In the same way, when the Believer, like a sheep, goes astray and gets wounded, and is on the verge of causing his or her own demise, without any judgment, God comes and anoints the wound for physical recovery and extends His mercy for spiritual healing.

---

[25] Daniël Francois O'Kennedy, "God as Healer in the Prophetic Books of the Hebrew Bible." *Horizons in Biblical Theology 27*, no. 1 (June 2005): 87–113.

CHAPTER EIGHT—THE ABUNDANCE OF ROYAL BLESSINGS

"My cup runs over." (v. 5c)

David is now expressing his exultation.

Another phase of God's restoration is the overflowing of His blessings to those under His care. Not only has God blessed him, but his cup has overflowed—representing the surplus and abundance of his tremendous life success.

The notion of the cup "running over" alludes to how God's blessings are always bestowed more exceedingly and more abundantly than anticipated. The generous and unstinting kingship of YHWH, a theme throughout both the Old and New Testament, is founded on His cosmic ownership.

As the King of kings, Creator, and Ruler of the universe, He owns "the cattle on a thousand hills." (Ps. 50:10)

"The silver *is* Mine, and the gold *is* Mine," says the Lord of hosts. (Hag. 2:8)

He makes the threshing floors full of grain, and the vats overflow with wine and oil. (Joel 2:24)

He is the giver of "good measure, pressed down, shaken together, and running over." (Luke 6:38)

As king, He can do exceedingly and abundantly more than His subjects could ever require because He is enthroned "above all that we ask, or think, according to the power that works in us." (Eph. 3:20)

Gottfried Voight explains that "king in the full sense can be said only of God and every earthly king is king only insofar as God's dignity bestowed upon him."[26] Human kingship in all its extravagance is only a meager image of the kingship of God.

Whereas worldly kingdoms rule by law and compulsion, God's kingdom is based on love and sacrifice; such royal characteristics allow Him to exalt those who humble themselves before Him, giving them more than they deserve.

In his royal portrayal of YHWH, David goes one step further in this verse, from "not lacking" to "overflowing." This progression is to say that where the shepherd metaphor comes with limitations, the royal imagery evokes unlimited blessings. It is my firm belief that every true Believer can express their own exultation in Christ as their King.

"Surely goodness and mercy shall follow me all the days of my life." (v. 6a)

The word for mercy in Hebrew is חֶסֶד (hessed) which can also be translated as "loving-kindness."

And the Hebrew verb for "follow" in this verse is רָדַף (radaf) which means to persecute or pursue. That is a rather sharp word used to describe God's loving-kindness. This word is the same one used when Joseph commanded the steward of his house to "follow" his brothers and "overtake them." (Gen. 44:4) This language suggests a retrospection of David's

---

[26]   Gottfried Voigt, "The Speaking Christ in His Royal Office." *Concordia Theological Monthly 23* (1952): 161–75.

life journey where he recalls how God's mercy accompanied and enveloped him under the pressure of persecution.

Throughout his life, David experienced God's relentless mercy חֶסֶד numerous times through a series of unforeseen events requiring the longsuffering attribute of YHWH.

He was a man of war, and under the sharp blade of his sword, many perished, resulting in God prohibiting him from building the Temple (1 Chro. 28:3).

And later on, during perhaps the second most well-known event in the life of David—his adulterous affair with Bathsheba, a host of sins would have been committed to further necessitate the mercy of God toward him (see 2 Sam. 11:1-27). In his contrition and lamentation of this wrongdoing, David cries out to God: "Have mercy on me, O God, according to כְּחַסְדֶּךָ *(ke·chas·de·cha)*," meaning "your loving-kindness." (Ps. 51:21) Hence, David understood quite clearly the unrelenting pursuit of God's mercy when he utilized the verb *radaf.*

The compassion of YHWH is one of His most compelling attributes. It refuses to let go of us. It is His compassion that attracts us to Him. His constant unmerited forgiveness compels us to surrender to Him. We turn our hearts toward God because He is so mindful and considerate of us. We love God because He first loved us. His shameful death on the cross in our stead persuades us of His love and mercy for us. Indeed, we are all beneficiaries of His relentless mercy from which derives our salvation.

Babatunde Ogunlana brilliantly says that "God's longsuffering means He endures and holds back judgment on sin to give sinners time to respond. Longsuffering is gracious in that those who respond rightly are saved."[27]

God is a just God, and He judges everyone accordingly. He is, however, as merciful as He is just. Thus, David is grateful for the loving-kindness of YHWH, and he is persuaded that such compassion will continue to be extended to him due to the unchanging nature of YHWH as his King.

27 Babatunde Ogunlana A., "God's Compassion in Jonah as Motivation for Christian Mission." *BTSK Insight 15,* no. 2 (October 2018): 172–200.

NOTES

It was believed that, as long as the Temple stood, and the name of YHWH is called upon in the Temple, it would be inviolable and the city infallible.

CHAPTER NINE—IN GRATITUDE TO THE KING

And I will dwell in the house of the Lord, forever." (v. 6b)

*I*n gratitude to the King-Host, David has vowed to dwell in His house forever. David has always been one to express gladness for the house of the Lord. "I was glad," David shouts, "when they said to me, 'Let us go into the house of the Lord.'" (Ps. 122:1) But now, he does not simply wish to go to Temple for service; instead, he hopes to dwell therein forever.

Scholars are not all in agreement with the meaning of verse 6b. Some arguments concerning this part of the verse are somewhat controversial.

For instance, Amado suggests that this imagery alludes to the cultic culture of Mesopotamia, where, in their god's temple, worshippers had dedicated statues to their gods, symbolizing their continual presence before those gods, ensuring their divine safety, goodness, and peace.[28]

"Dwelling in the house of the Lord," also resembles the inviolability theology in Jerusalem at the time of Jeremiah when the Temple stood as a symbol of safety. It was believed that,

---

[28]   David Adamo T., "Reading Psalm 23 in African Context." *Verbum et Ecclesia 39,* no. 1 (January 2018), 1–8.

as long as the Temple stood, and the name of YHWH is called upon in the Temple, it would be inviolable and the city infallible. Hence, every worshipper desired to dwell in the Temple. It is quite possible that the Psalmist was well aware of that notion.

Tappy goes in a different direction in saying that David is nowhere suggesting that he would dedicate himself to serving out his days in the temple priesthood. The statement is rather an idiomatic reference to YHWH's temple, based on the kinship structure of the Israelite society at a local level, where the house of the father *(bet. Ab)* constitutes the underlying unit of village organization.[29] Dwelling in an earthly father's house whether that title is acquired biologically, matrimonially, or even through fictive adoption, meant sharing in that family's patrimony or inheritance.

Though both arguments, regardless of how diametrically opposed they may be, are plausible, I tend to lean towards the latter. I personally identify with Tappy's argument based on its paternalistic approach.

I have been living away from my biological father since I was an adolescent. Not because he is a deadbeat dad, or there was any problem in the family, but rather, because of the incommodious circumstances of life. (Perhaps I will elaborate on that if I ever write an autobiography). Since I have been living away from my biological father all these years, growing up, I had many father figures in my life. They came at various stages of my life.

But there is one particular father figure with whom I am close to this day. Although he has never legally adopted me, we are truly family. Whenever I visit his house, whether I stay for two weeks or two months, I am treated as family. No payments required! How he lives, I live. What he eats, I eat. Where he stays, I stay. Su casa, mi casa!

---

[29] Ron Tappy E, "Psalm 23: Symbolism and Structure." *The Catholic Biblical Quarterly 57*, no. 2 (April 1995), 255–80.

In my case, it does not get as far as Tappy proposes in sonship being part of the "family's patrimony or inheritance," nor do I seek such; however, as far as he and I are concerned, we are father and son. It is a fictive sonship, but sonship, nonetheless.

Let us now briefly consider the word *forever*. The Hebrew words translated into forever here, are לְאֹרֶךְ יָמִים (*lə·'ō·reḵ yā·mîm, read in Hebrew from right to left*) which could also be translated as "length of time or length of days." What is worth noticing is that the length of time is not specified. Although it is translated as "forever," it could very well mean for the remainder of his days or eternity or both. In which case, Tappy's argument works best because David cannot physically "dwell" in the temple for "eternity."

Going back to my scenario, my fictive father remains a father to me forever, meaning for the duration of his days here on earth. On the other hand, I have been grafted into the family permanently, or even *beyond* the course of his days.

In that context, David may be conveying his sonship through worship.

When believers worship God in church, we recognize that God's presence is there with us in the atmosphere. We know this because Psalm 22:3 tells us that YHWH is "enthroned in the praises" of His people. David knew it too; he wrote Psalm 22. Using the phrase "dwelling in the house of the Lord forever," David could be referring to the abiding spiritual presence of YHWH during corporate worship in the earthly temple, which is a precursor of the ever-abiding physical presence of YHWH in heaven.

Moreover, God created us to worship Him. (Is. 43:7) The Bible clarifies that we are the Temple of God; (1 Cor. 3:16-17) once we remain in a covenant relationship with God, we will dwell in His presence—perpetually. Wherever we may be, whether, in the earthly or heavenly tabernacle, the omnipresence of YHWH abides in and with us all, forever.

"Forever" further suggests an everlasting inheritance. As the King-Host, YHWH prepares a lavish banquet in David's honor to make their covenant relationship public. The initial reception, in the form of the public feast, also means that he has been accepted and adopted into the family of YHWH. Through this adoption, David is immediately heir to an everlasting inheritance which he may enjoy in his days here on earth and in the life to come after his resurrection at the Second Coming of the Messiah King.

Ultimately, the progression of David's relationship with YHWH—from the imagery of the divine caring Shepherd to the inviting King-Host, suggests that David is entirely accepted through "spiritual adoption" into the kinship structure of the sociological term *bet-ab* (the father's house).

Whether Amado or Tappy's view is adopted, the conclusive evidence in the Poem exhibits that David is so pleased with YHWH's tender care and royal treatment that he vows to remain in the presence of his paternal King-Host for the remainder of his days, here on earth and in the life to come.

YHWH's adoption of David is good news to Believers, especially those who are fatherless, to know that they, too, may be spiritually adopted into the royal family of YHWH as well.

Those who worship God in spirit and in truth are, in fact, children of God. When we dwell in the presence of YHWH through worship, we feel a sense of belonging in the fellowship of God's children, and His presence surrounds us as a hedge of protection, keeping us safe from intruders. As children of YHWH, we are not adopted for a limited time. Our adoption does not expire after 18 years or when we are married—it is forever. Thus, like David, we may also dwell in the house of the Lord forever as His sons and daughters through our worship.

PRAYING IN PSALM 23

Prayer #6

Yahweh is my Shepherd;

The Hope of my glory.

Yahweh is my Shepherd;

Forever, Him and me.

NOTES

SECTION THREE

SUMMARY

Psalm 23 is the most well-known Psalm of the entire OT by both Christians and non-Christians. It is usually recited in moments of distress and as part of liturgical worship. Unlike the Shepherd metaphor, the King-Host metaphor is often oblivious or utterly omitted in the Poem. Many scholarly writings focus on the Shepherd metaphor while neglecting or omitting the King-Host imagery.

The authorship of the Psalm is superscripted to David who himself was shepherd and king. David wrote the Poem from the perspective of a sheep and not the shepherd. He commences the Psalm with an exclamation, "YHWH is my shepherd," which serves as the engine for the entire Psalm.

David uses the shepherd metaphor as shepherding played a central role in ancient Israel and the reader would have imagined the shepherd tending the sheep and leading the people. In the ancient Near East, gods and kings were considered shepherds as well.

The bucolic and colorful imagery in the Poem depicts the Shepherd as a good shepherd who only leads His sheep to green pastures for grazing and ruminating, and to tranquil waters that quench their thirst. In that mindset, David expresses: "I shall not want," to say that YHWH provides for his every need.

As aforementioned, Clines notes that while it is not wrong to translate אֶחְסָר: (want) in the future tense, a better translation would be "I do not lack," since the author is expressing his present state.

YHWH, the Shepherd, does not lead the sheep in straight paths only to save His reputation, but because that is just who He is. His character would not allow Him to do otherwise. Even when the sheep go astray and are wounded, the Shepherd restores them to the ideal condition. He is as concerned with the sheep that are lost as He is with the ones that are not.

People learn primarily through experience, and from the matrix of David's own experience with sheep, he trusts the Shepherd for the fact that He would not lead him on a road where he had not been before. Therefore, though he would walk through any dark alley or experience any level of evil, he does not fear such desperate situations because the presence of God, his Shepherd, is with him.

In verse 4c, David uses two words "rod and staff" which could be used interchangeably; except in verse 5a, David introduces another persona of the Shepherd, likening Him unto a King-Host who prepares a table in honor of David in the presence of his enemies. The wordplay opens up the possibility of intentionality on David's part that perhaps he intended for his readers to notice the paradigm shift in the Psalm.

The mentioning of a table set for David in the presence of his "enemies" suggests a sign of judgment on the enemies of YHWH, the King-Host, who taunt His followers asking, "where is your God?"

Hence, YHWH lavishes David, His guest, with a meal feast as a sign of honor and alliance, letting the enemies know that the King is ready to defend and protect His subject at all costs. In gratitude to his paternal King-Host, David vows always to be loyal to YHWH and never leave His sight, by promising to dwell in His house forever.

NOTES

CONCLUSION

In the 23rd Psalm, it is not two different YHWHs depicted, but rather the same God whose glory fills the entire cosmos, and who is yet, able to simultaneously make Himself so minute that He may dwell in each of our hearts, hence— Emmanuel, God with us.

The role or title "shepherd" was indeed used to describe the role of leaders and their relationship to the people in their charge; however, the work of a shepherd was a lowly job. While shepherding was a common job, being a shepherd was an intimate ministry, in part because of the long durations that shepherds spent in the company of their sheep.

Thus, Christ came to this earth and made Himself as low as we, His sheep, are so that He might save us. And through the Holy Spirit, He can spend aeons with us. For this reason, He has promised to never leave nor forsake us and to always be with us no matter the circumstances. (Matt. 28:20; Jn 14:18)

Jesus knows our every need. We can trust Him for anywhere with Jesus we can safely go.

Christ is the meek and lowly Shepherd and yet, He is also the high and mighty King. It is in this mindset that David exclaims: "I shall not want!"

This language does not suggest mere material prosperity as some may conclude; instead, it offers immeasurable spiritual benefits that are found only in Jesus.

David purposely transitions from the shepherd metaphor to royal imagery whereas the view of the shepherd seems inadequate and limited, the king-host metaphor offers endless power and possibilities of blessings. Psalm 23 is good news to the Believer. He or she who has accepted Jesus Christ as his or her Lord and Savior, may make the same claim as David. Jesus labels Himself the "Good Shepherd," but also the "King of kings," and "Lord of lords." These attributes are reassuring in that they offer a sense of security that is found in no one else.

The correlative metaphors employed in the Poem present God as truly the Alpha and Omega. The author starts with YHWH—YHWH is my shepherd (v. 1) and ends with YHWH—I will dwell in the House of YHWH (v. 6) to form a beautiful *inclusio*, portraying the Lord as his *all in all*. The depiction of YHWH progresses from Shepherd to King. The faith-based premises established in the Psalm, through royal imagery, convince us that we, too, can trust the capability of YHWH as our King in every situation for the reason that there is no limit to His dispensing power.

In light of the current events happening all over the world (i.e., the COVID-19 Pandemic ravaging the globe; the political unrests in many parts of the world; and the fulfillment of the Last Days' events as predicted in Matthew 24 and elsewhere in the Holy Bible), we are reminded that the Lord is our Shepherd, and He is with us even in these dark times.

As time progresses, even more evil will befall the world. At the rate of the occurrences of recent catastrophes, the state of the world will inevitably worsen before experiencing permanent peace through the everlasting reign of our Shepherd-King, Jesus Christ.

Meanwhile, rather than falling into a perennial paralysis caused by fear, let us stand on the promises of God, such as the one made to Joshua in Deut. 31:8, "The Lord Himself goes before you and will be with you; He will never leave you nor forsake you. Do not be afraid; do not be discouraged."

Therefore, let us not fear any evil!

Not now, not ever!

"For God has not given us a spirit of fear, but of power and of love and of a sound mind." (2 Tim 1:7) We may not know what the future holds, but we are confident that YHWH holds the future.

He is in control, and He has a perfect plan.

We hurt, yet we hope! We cry, still we rejoice!

For "weeping may endure for a night, but joy *comes* in the morning." (Ps.30:5)

Thus, while YHWH shepherds us, we know He is present in our midst through the Holy Spirit even though we cannot see Him.

Furthermore, in addition to His abiding spiritual presence, we rest on the promise that Christ will soon establish His physical Messianic Kingdom which shall last forever; and ALL who truly love and trust Him until the end will, at last, behold Him face-to-face and harmoniously dwell in His house forever!

What a day of rejoicing that will be!

Even so, come Lord Jesus. Amen!

NOTES

Prayers/Poem on Psalm 23:

Prayer/Stanza #1

Yahweh is my Shepherd,
Thus, all my needs are met;
Yahweh is my Shepherd,
Henceforth, I shall not fret.

Prayer/Stanza #2

Yahweh is my Shepherd,
My Load has been carried;
Yahweh is my Shepherd,
Hence, I am not worried.

Prayer/Stanza #4

Yahweh is my Shepherd,
So, I am not alone;
Yahweh is my Shepherd,
And that is set in stone!

Prayer/Stanza #5

Yahweh is my Shepherd,
He shall conquer my foe;
Yahweh is my Shepherd,
He's my Superhero!

Prayer/Stanza #3

Yahweh is my Shepherd,
He is my Hope and Stay;
Yahweh is my Shepherd,
He leads me all the way.

Prayer/Stanza #6

Yahweh is my Shepherd,
The Hope of my glory;
Yahweh is my Shepherd,
Forever, Him and me.

BIBLIOGRAPHY

Adamo, David T. "Reading Psalm 23 in African Context." *Verbum et Ecclesia* 39, no. 1 (January 2018): 1–8.

Bergant, Dianne. *Psalms 1-72 : Volume 22. New Collegeville Bible Commentary. Old Testament.* Collegeville, Minnesota: Liturgical Press, 2013.

Blasa, Erwin, and Clarence Marquez. "Towards A 'Shepherd' Spirituality: The Application of the Image of Sheep-and-Shepherd in Psalm 23 to Seminary Formation in the Philippines." *Philippiniana Sacra* 45, no. 135 (September 2010): 610–70.

Clines, David J. A. "The Lord Is My Shepherd in East and South East Asia." *Sino- Christian Studies 1* (June 2006): 37–54.

Coronation." *Columbia Electronic Encyclopedia, 6th Edition*, February 2020, 1.

Goulder, Michael. "David and Yahweh in Psalms 23 and 24." *Journal for the Study of the Old Testament 30,* no. 4 (June 2006): 463–73.

Gunkel, Hermann. *The Psalms: A Form-Critical Introduction.* Tubingen: Fortress Press, 1967.

Keller, Phillip W. A Shepherd's Look At Psalm 23. Grand Rapids, MI: Zondervan Publishing House, 1970-71.

Klingbeil, Martin G. "Psalm 23." Seventh-day Adventist International Bible Commentary [in print].

Mayes, James L. *Psalms-Interpretation-A Bible Commentary for Teaching and Preaching.* John Louisville: Knox Press, [1994].

Muthunayagom, Daniel Jones. "The Image of God as King and the Nature of His Power in the Old Testament." *Bangalore Theological Forum* 41, no. 2 (2009): 29–48.

Nel, Philip J. "Yahweh Is a Shepherd: Conceptual Metaphor in Psalm 23." *Horizons in Biblical Theology* 27, no. 2 (December 2005): 79–103.

O'Kennedy, Daniël Francois. "God as Healer in the Prophetic Books of the Hebrew Bible." *Horizons in Biblical Theology* 27, no. 1 (June 2005): 87–113.Steussy, Marti J. *David : Biblical Portraits of Power.* Studies on Personalities of the Old Testament. Columbia, S.C.: University of South Carolina Press, 1999. 40-41.

Ogunlana, Babatunde A. "God's Compassion in Jonah as Motivation for Christian Mission." *BTSK Insight 15,* no. 2 (October 2018): 172–200.

Steussy, Marti J. *David : Biblical Portraits of Power. Studies on Personalities of the Old Testament.* (Columbia, S.C.: University of South Carolina Press, 1999), 41-42.

Tappy, Ron E. "Psalm 23: Symbolism and Structure." *The Catholic Biblical Quarterly 57,* no. 2 (April 1995): 255–80.

Thorpe, Jacqulyn Brown. "Psalm 23: A Remix." *Journal of Religious Thought 59/60,* no. 1/2, 1 (January 2006): 165–79.

Voigt, Gottfried. "The Speaking Christ in His Royal Office." Concordia Theological Monthly 23 (1952), 161–75.

Wilson, Gerald H., *The NIV Application Commentary, Psalm Vol. 1,* (Zondervan, Grand Rapids, MI, 2002), 434.

Printed in the United States
by Baker & Taylor Publisher Services